Betty Crocker®

20 best
doughnut recipes

Houghton Mifflin Harcourt
Boston • New York • 2013

Cover photo: Snickerdoodle Mini Doughnuts (page 14)

General Mills
Food Content and Relationship Marketing Director: Geoff Johnson
Food Content Marketing Manager: Susan Klobuchar
Senior Editor: Grace Wells
Kitchen Manager: Ann Stuart
Recipe Development and Testing: Betty Crocker Kitchens
Photography: General Mills Photography Studios and Image Library

Houghton Mifflin Harcourt
Publisher: Natalie Chapman
Editorial Director: Cindy Kitchel
Executive Editor: Anne Ficklen
Associate Editor: Heather Dabah
Managing Editor: Rebecca Springer
Production Editor: Kristi Hart
Cover Design: Chrissy Kurpeski
Book Design: Tai Blanche

ISBN 978-0-544-31476-4
Printed in the United States of America

The Betty Crocker Kitchens seal guarantees success in your kitchen. Every recipe has been tested in America's Most Trusted Kitchens™ to meet our high standards of reliability, easy preparation and great taste.

FIND MORE GREAT IDEAS AT
Betty Crocker.com

Dear Friends,

This new collection of colorful mini books has been put together with you in mind because we know that you love great recipes and enjoy cooking and baking but have a busy lifestyle. So every little book in the series contains just 20 recipes for you to treasure and enjoy. Plus, each book is a single subject designed in a bite-size format just for you—it's easy to use and is filled with favorite recipes from the Betty Crocker Kitchens!

All of the books are conveniently divided into short chapters so you can quickly find what you're looking for, and the beautiful photos throughout are sure to entice you into making the delicious recipes. In the series, you'll discover a fabulous array of recipes to spark your interest—from cookies, cupcakes and birthday cakes to party ideas for a variety of occasions. There's grilled foods, potluck favorites and even gluten-free recipes too.

You'll love the variety in these mini books—so pick one or choose them all for your cooking pleasure.

Enjoy and happy cooking!

Sincerely,

Betty Crocker

contents

Baked Sugar Doughnuts

Prep Time: 15 Minutes • **Start to Finish:** 30 Minutes • Makes 10 doughnuts and 10 centers

1 can (7.5 oz) refrigerated
  buttermilk biscuits

3 tablespoons butter or
  margarine, melted

⅓ cup sugar

1 Heat oven to 375°F.

2 Separate dough into 10 biscuits; flatten each to
2½-inch round. Using 1-inch round biscuit cutter, cut
hole in center of each round. Dip all sides of biscuits and
centers into butter, then into sugar. Place on ungreased
cookie sheet.

3 Bake 12 to 14 minutes or until golden brown.

1 Doughnut and 1 Center: Calories 110; Total Fat 4g (Saturated Fat 2g, Trans
Fat 0g); Cholesterol 10mg; Sodium 210mg; Total Carbohydrate 16g (Dietary
Fiber 0g); Protein 1g **Exchanges:** ½ Starch, ½ Other Carbohydrate, 1 Fat
Carbohydrate Choices: 1

Tip Drizzle a thin chocolate glaze over baked and
cooled doughnuts for a decadent, delicious treat!

Applesauce Doughnuts

Prep Time: 40 Minutes • **Start to Finish:** 1 Hour 40 Minutes • Makes 18 doughnuts

3 ⅓ cups Gold Medal®
  all-purpose flour

1 cup applesauce

¾ cup sugar

2 tablespoons shortening

3 teaspoons baking powder

1 teaspoon ground cinnamon

½ teaspoon salt

2 eggs

Vegetable oil for deep frying

Cinnamon-sugar mixture, if
  desired

1 In large bowl, beat 1⅓ cups of the flour and all remaining ingredients except oil and cinnamon-sugar with electric mixer on low speed, scraping bowl constantly, until blended. Beat on medium speed 2 minutes, scraping bowl occasionally. Stir in remaining 2 cups flour. Cover and refrigerate about 1 hour or until dough stiffens.

2 In deep fryer or 3-quart saucepan, heat 2 to 3 inches oil to 375°F. Divide dough in half. On generously floured cloth-covered surface, place half of the dough; gently roll in flour to coat. Gently roll dough to ⅜-inch thickness. Cut with floured doughnut cutter. Repeat with remaining half of dough.

3 Using wide spatula, slide 2 or 3 doughnuts at a time into hot oil. Turn doughnuts as they rise to surface. Fry 1 to 1½ minutes on each side or until golden brown. Carefully remove from oil (do not prick surfaces); drain on paper towels. Sprinkle hot doughnuts with cinnamon-sugar.

1 Doughnut: Calories 230; Total Fat 11g (Saturated Fat 2g. Trans Fat 0g); Cholesterol 20mg; Sodium 150mg; Total Carbohydrate 29g (Dietary Fiber 1g); Protein 3g **Exchanges:** 1 Starch, 1 Other Carbohydrate, 2 Fat **Carbohydrate Choices:** 2

Tip Like your doughnuts completely coated? Add the cinnamon-sugar to a plastic or paper bag, and shake one or two doughnuts at a time in the mixture until coated.

Coffee-Glazed Doughnuts

Prep Time: 40 Minutes • **Start to Finish:** 2 Hours 30 Minutes • Makes 34 doughnuts

1 package regular active dry yeast

⅓ cup granulated sugar

2 tablespoons warm water (105°F to 115°F)

¾ cup warm milk (105°F to 115°F)

3 tablespoons butter, softened

½ teaspoon salt

1 egg

3 cups Gold Medal all-purpose flour

4 teaspoons instant coffee granules or crystals

¼ cup boiling water

3 cups powdered sugar

1 tablespoon light corn syrup

¼ teaspoon vanilla

⅛ teaspoon salt

Vegetable oil for deep frying

Assorted colored candy sprinkles

1 In large bowl, mix yeast and 1 teaspoon of the granulated sugar. Add warm water; let stand 5 minutes or until foamy. Add remaining granulated sugar, the warm milk, butter, ½ teaspoon salt, the egg and 1 cup of the flour; beat with electric mixer on low speed 30 seconds. Beat on medium speed 2 minutes. Beat in 1½ cups of the flour, ¼ cup at a time, until dough no longer sticks to bowl. (Dough will be soft.)

2 On lightly floured surface, knead dough about 5 minutes, sprinkling remaining ½ cup flour over surface if dough starts to stick, until dough is smooth and springy. Grease large bowl with shortening or cooking spray. Place dough in bowl, turning dough to grease all sides. Cover loosely with plastic wrap and cloth towel. Let rise in warm place (80°F to 85°F) 1 hour or until doubled in size. Gently push fist into dough to deflate. On lightly floured surface, roll dough to ½-inch thickness. Cut dough using 2-inch round cutter, rerolling dough once; cut out centers using ¾-inch round cutter. On ungreased cookie sheets, place doughnuts and holes about 1 inch apart; cover and let rise 45 minutes or until doubled in size.

3 Meanwhile, in medium bowl, dissolve coffee granules in boiling water. Add powdered sugar, corn syrup, vanilla and ⅛ teaspoon salt; beat with whisk until blended and smooth. Set aside.

4 In deep fryer or heavy saucepan, heat 2½ inches oil to 350°F. Fry doughnuts and holes in batches in hot oil about 1 minute on each side or until golden brown. Remove from oil with slotted spoon; drain on paper towels. Dip doughnuts (and holes, if desired) into coffee glaze, turning until completely coated. Sprinkle with candy sprinkles before glaze sets. Place on cooling racks until set.

1 Doughnut: Calories 121; Total Fat 4g (Saturated Fat 1g, Trans Fat 0g); Cholesterol 0g; Sodium 58mg; Total Carbohydrate 21g (Dietary Fiber 0g); Protein 2g **Exchanges:** ½ Starch, 1 Other Carbohydrate, ½ Fat **Carbohydrate Choices:** 1½

Tip Instead of the coffee glaze, dip the doughnuts and holes into cinnamon-sugar.

Baked Blueberry-Orange Doughnuts

Prep Time: 25 Minutes · **Start to Finish:** 40 Minutes · Makes 12 doughnuts

Streusel

3 tablespoons Gold Medal all-purpose flour

3 tablespoons sugar

1 tablespoon butter or margarine

3 tablespoons sliced almonds

½ teaspoon grated orange peel

Doughnuts

½ cup butter or margarine, softened

⅔ cup sugar

2 eggs

¼ cup milk

¼ cup freshly squeezed orange juice

2 cups Gold Medal all-purpose flour

2 teaspoons grated orange peel

1½ teaspoons baking powder

½ teaspoon salt

¾ cup fresh blueberries

1 Heat oven to 425°F. Lightly spray 2 regular-size doughnut pans (6 doughnuts per pan) with cooking spray.

2 In small bowl, mix 3 tablespoons flour and 3 tablespoons sugar. Cut in 1 tablespoon butter, using pastry blender or fork, until mixture is crumbly. Stir in remaining streusel ingredients; set aside.

3 In medium bowl, beat ½ cup butter, ⅔ cup sugar and the eggs with electric mixer on medium speed until smooth. Add milk and orange juice; beat on low speed until well mixed. Stir in 2 cups flour, 2 teaspoons orange peel, the baking powder and salt just until flour is moistened. Fold in blueberries.

4 Spoon batter evenly into doughnut pans, filling wells about ¼ inch from top of pan; sprinkle with streusel. Bake 6 to 8 minutes or until toothpick inserted in center comes out clean. Cool 5 minutes; remove from pan to cooling rack. Serve warm or cool.

1 Doughnut: Calories 250; Total Fat 11g (Saturated Fat 6g, Trans Fat 0g); Cholesterol 55mg; Sodium 250mg; Total Carbohydrate 34g (Dietary Fiber 1g); Protein 4g **Exchanges:** 1 Starch, 1½ Other Carbohydrate, 2 Fat **Carbohydrate Choices:** 2

Tip Small blueberries work best for this recipe because you'll get more berries in each doughnut, but if your berries are large, the doughnuts will be just as delicious!

Baked Banana–Chocolate Chip Doughnuts

Prep Time: 25 Minutes • **Start to Finish:** 40 Minutes • Makes 16 doughnuts

Doughnuts

½ cup butter or margarine, softened

⅔ cup granulated sugar

2 eggs

1½ cups mashed very ripe bananas (3 medium)

1 teaspoon vanilla

2¼ cups Gold Medal all-purpose flour

1½ teaspoons baking powder

½ teaspoon salt

½ cup miniature semisweet chocolate chips

Glaze

1 cup powdered sugar

½ cup caramel topping

4 to 5 teaspoons whipping cream

Garnish

Dried banana chips, chopped, if desired

1 Heat oven to 425°F. Lightly spray 2 regular-size doughnut pans (6 doughnuts per pan) with cooking spray.

2 In medium bowl, beat butter, granulated sugar and eggs with electric mixer on medium speed until smooth. Add bananas and vanilla; beat on low speed until well mixed. Stir in flour, baking powder and salt just until flour is moistened. Stir in chocolate chips.

3 Spoon batter evenly into doughnut pans, filling wells about ¼ inch from top of pan. (Refrigerate remaining batter for remaining doughnuts. Cool pan before baking remaining doughnuts.) Bake 6 to 8 minutes or until toothpick inserted in center comes out clean. Cool 5 minutes; carefully remove from pan to cooling rack.

4 Meanwhile, in small bowl, mix all glaze ingredients until well blended. Dip top of each doughnut into glaze or drizzle with glaze; sprinkle with banana chips. Serve warm or cool.

1 Doughnut: Calories 270; Total Fat 9g (Saturated Fat 5g, Trans Fat 0g); Cholesterol 40mg; Sodium 220mg; Total Carbohydrate 45g (Dietary Fiber 1g); Protein 3g **Exchanges:** 1 Starch, 2 Other Carbohydrate, 1½ Fat **Carbohydrate Choices:** 3

Tip Miniature semisweet chocolate chips are the best choice because they won't sink in the batter and you get more chips in each bite!

Double Berry Doughnuts

Prep Time: 25 Minutes • **Start to Finish:** 1 Hour • Makes 12 doughnuts

2 cups Original Bisquick® mix
¼ cup granulated sugar
⅔ cup milk
2½ teaspoons vanilla
1 egg
½ cup dried blueberries
½ cup frozen raspberries (do not thaw)
2 tablespoons water
2 cups powdered sugar
4½ teaspoons milk

1 Heat oven to 425°F. Lightly spray 2 regular-size doughnut pans (6 doughnuts per pan) with cooking spray. In medium bowl, stir Bisquick mix, 2 tablespoons of the granulated sugar, ⅔ cup milk, 2 teaspoons of the vanilla and the egg until blended. Stir in blueberries. Spoon batter into resealable food-storage plastic bag; seal bag. Cut off small corner of bag; squeeze bag to pipe batter into pan, using about ¼ cup for each doughnut.

2 Bake 7 to 9 minutes or until toothpick inserted near center comes out clean. Immediately remove from pan to cooling rack. Cool completely, about 30 minutes.

3 In 1-quart saucepan, heat raspberries, water and remaining 2 tablespoons granulated sugar to boiling over medium heat. Cook 2 to 3 minutes longer or until thickened and syrupy. Strain; cool. Stir in 1 cup of the powdered sugar and the remaining ½ teaspoon vanilla with whisk until smooth and thickened. Dip top of each doughnut into berry glaze; let excess drip off. Let stand until set.

4 In medium bowl, mix remaining 1 cup powdered sugar and 4½ teaspoons milk with whisk until smooth. Drizzle over doughnuts. Let stand until set.

1 Doughnut: Calories 230; Total Fat 3.5g (Saturated Fat 1g, Trans Fat 0g); Cholesterol 0mg; Sodium 260mg; Total Carbohydrate 48g (Dietary Fiber 2g); Protein 3g **Exchanges:** 1 Starch, 2 Other Carbohydrate, ½ Fat **Carbohydrate Choices:** 3

Caramel-Pretzel Doughnuts

Prep Time: 20 Minutes • **Start to Finish:** 45 Minutes • Makes 12 doughnuts

⅓ cup butter or margarine

⅔ cup packed brown sugar

¼ cup milk

2 cups Original Bisquick mix

2 tablespoons granulated sugar

⅔ cup milk

1 teaspoon vanilla

1 egg

2 tablespoons butter, melted

½ cup powdered sugar

1 cup small pretzel twists, broken

⅓ cup flaked coconut

1 Heat oven to 425°F. Lightly spray 2 regular-size doughnut pans (6 doughnuts per pan) with cooking spray. In 2-quart saucepan, melt ⅓ cup butter over medium heat. Stir in brown sugar. Heat to boiling, stirring constantly. Stir in 3 tablespoons of the milk; return to boiling. Remove from heat; cool to room temperature.

2 Meanwhile, in medium bowl, stir Bisquick mix, granulated sugar, ⅔ cup milk, the vanilla and egg until blended. Stir in 2 tablespoons butter. Spoon batter into resealable food-storage plastic bag; seal bag. Cut off small corner of bag; squeeze bag to pipe batter into pan, using about ¼ cup for each doughnut.

3 Bake 7 to 9 minutes or until toothpick inserted near center comes out clean. Immediately remove from pan to cooling rack; cool completely, about 15 minutes.

4 Gradually beat powdered sugar into brown sugar mixture with whisk until smooth, adding remaining 1 tablespoon milk if needed. Glaze doughnuts; sprinkle with pretzels and coconut.

1 Doughnut: Calories 260; Total Fat 11g (Saturated Fat 6g, Trans Fat 0g); Cholesterol 0mg; Sodium 410mg; Total Carbohydrate 39g (Dietary Fiber 0g); Protein 3g **Exchanges:** 1 Starch, 1½ Other Carbohydrate, 2 Fat **Carbohydrate Choices:** 2½

Apple-Cinnamon Doughnut Bites

Prep Time: 25 Minutes • **Start to Finish:** 25 Minutes • Makes 32 doughnut bites

Vegetable oil for deep frying

¼ cup sugar

½ teaspoon ground cinnamon

½ cup apple pie filling (from 21-oz can)

1 can (12.4 oz) refrigerated cinnamon rolls with icing

1 In deep fryer or 3-quart heavy saucepan, heat 2 to 3 inches oil to 375°F. In small bowl, mix sugar and cinnamon; set aside.

2 In food processor, place apple pie filling. Cover; process, using quick on-and-off motions, 10 to 20 seconds or until pureed.

3 Set aside icing from cinnamon rolls. Separate dough into 8 rolls; cut each roll into quarters. Fry in batches in hot oil 1 to 2 minutes or until golden brown on all sides. Remove from oil with slotted spoon; drain on paper towels. Immediately roll in cinnamon-sugar mixture.

4 Place apple mixture in decorating bag fitted with small round tip #10. Insert tip into side of each doughnut; pipe small amount of apple mixture into doughnut.

5 In small microwavable bowl, heat reserved icing on High 10 to 20 seconds until thin enough to drizzle. Drizzle icing over doughnuts. Serve warm.

1 Doughnut Bite: Calories 127; Total Fat 11g (Saturated Fat 1g, Trans Fat 0g); Cholesterol 0mg; Sodium 87mg; Total Carbohydrate 8g (Dietary Fiber 0g); Protein 1g **Exchanges:** ½ Other Carbohydrate, 2 Fat **Carbohydrate Choices:** ½

Snickerdoodle Mini Doughnuts

Prep Time: 45 Minutes · **Start to Finish:** 2 Hours · Makes 26 mini doughnuts

Doughnuts

⅓ cup sugar

¼ cup butter, melted

2 eggs

⅓ cup milk

3 tablespoons sour cream

1 teaspoon vanilla

2 cups Gold Medal all-purpose flour

1½ teaspoons ground cinnamon

1 teaspoon cream of tartar

1 teaspoon baking powder

Topping

¾ cup sugar

3 tablespoons ground cinnamon

6 tablespoons butter, melted

1 In medium bowl, mix ⅓ cup sugar, ¼ cup butter and the eggs until smooth. Stir in milk, sour cream and vanilla with whisk. Stir in flour, 1½ teaspoons cinnamon, the cream of tartar and baking powder just until moistened.

2 Grease medium bowl with shortening. Place dough in bowl, turning dough to grease all sides. Cover bowl with plastic wrap; refrigerate 1 hour.

3 Heat oven to 450°F. Line 2 cookie sheets with cooking parchment paper. Place dough on generously floured surface. Roll dough in flour to coat. With floured rolling pin, roll dough to ½-inch thickness. Cut dough using floured 1¾-inch round cookie cutter. Place dough rounds on cookie sheets about 1 inch apart. Cut out centers using floured ¾-inch round cookie cutter. Reroll scraps to cut additional doughnuts.

4 Bake 8 to 10 minutes or until edges just turn light golden brown. Immediately remove from cookie sheet to cooling rack. Cool 3 minutes.

5 In small bowl, stir ¾ cup sugar and 3 tablespoons cinnamon. Place 6 tablespoons butter in another small bowl. Quickly dip both sides of each warm doughnut into butter; let excess drip off. Using spoon, roll each doughnut in cinnamon-sugar mixture to coat. Return doughnuts to cooling rack. Serve warm.

1 Mini Doughnut: Calories 120; Total Fat 5g (Saturated Fat 3g, Trans Fat 0g); Cholesterol 30mg; Sodium 60mg; Total Carbohydrate 17g (Dietary Fiber 1g); Protein 1g **Exchanges:** ½ Starch, ½ Other Carbohydrate, 1 Fat **Carbohydrate Choices:** 1

Tip Refrigerating the dough makes it easier to roll, but extra flour is still needed to keep the dough from sticking to the work surface and rolling pin. Shake off any excess flour before placing the dough rounds on the cookie sheet.

Indian-Spiced Mini Doughnuts

Prep Time: 15 Minutes • **Start to Finish:** 45 Minutes • Makes 24 mini doughnuts

⅓ cup butter

1½ cups sugar

1 egg

1½ cups Gold Medal all-purpose flour

1½ teaspoons baking powder

½ teaspoon salt

¼ teaspoon ground nutmeg

¼ teaspoon ground ginger

½ cup milk

1 teaspoon ground cinnamon

1 teaspoon garam masala

¼ teaspoon ground cardamom

½ cup butter, melted

1 Heat oven to 350°F. Grease 24 mini muffin cups.

2 In large bowl, beat ⅓ cup butter, ½ cup of the sugar and the egg with electric mixer on medium speed until blended. In medium bowl, mix flour, baking powder, salt, nutmeg and ginger. Add flour mixture alternately with milk to butter mixture until blended. Divide batter evenly among muffin cups.

3 Bake 15 to 18 minutes or until light golden brown. Cool 5 minutes. Remove from pan to cooling rack.

4 In large resealable food-storage plastic bag, mix remaining 1 cup sugar, the cinnamon, garam masala and cardamom. Roll hot muffins in ½ cup melted butter, then toss in sugar mixture to coat. Serve warm.

1 Mini Doughnut: Calories 140; Total Fat 7g (Saturated Fat 4g, Trans Fat 0g); Cholesterol 25mg; Sodium 130mg; Total Carbohydrate 19g (Dietary Fiber 0g); Protein 1g **Exchanges:** 1½ Other Carbohydrate, 1 Fat **Carbohydrate Choices:** 1

Doughnut Holes

Prep Time: 45 Minutes • **Start to Finish:** 45 Minutes • Makes 24 doughnut holes

Vegetable oil for deep frying
¼ cup granulated sugar
½ teaspoon ground cinnamon
1¼ cups Bisquick® Gluten
  Free mix
¼ cup packed brown sugar
¼ teaspoon ground nutmeg
2 tablespoons butter, melted
⅓ cup buttermilk
1 egg, beaten

1 In deep fryer or 2-quart heavy saucepan, heat 2 to 3 inches oil to 375°F. In small bowl, mix granulated sugar and cinnamon; set aside.

2 In medium bowl, mix remaining ingredients until smooth. Shape dough into 24 (1¼-inch) balls. Carefully drop balls, 5 or 6 at a time, into hot oil. Fry about 1 to 2 minutes or until golden brown on all sides. Remove from oil with slotted spoon; drain on paper towels. Immediately roll in cinnamon-sugar mixture.

1 Doughnut Hole: Calories 60; Total Fat 2g (Saturated Fat 1g, Trans Fat 0g); Cholesterol 10mg; Sodium 85mg; Total Carbohydrate 10g (Dietary Fiber 0g); Protein 0g **Exchanges:** ½ Starch, ½ Fat **Carbohydrate Choices:** ½

Tip If you don't have buttermilk on hand, mix 1 teaspoon distilled white vinegar in ⅓ cup milk. Let stand 5 minutes.

Buttons and Bows

Prep Time: 15 Minutes • **Start to Finish:** 25 Minutes • Makes 8 buttons and bows

2 cups Original Bisquick mix

2 tablespoons sugar

1 teaspoon ground nutmeg

⅛ teaspoon ground cinnamon

⅓ cup milk

1 egg

¼ cup butter or margarine, melted

½ cup sugar

1 Heat oven to 400°F. In medium bowl, stir Bisquick mix, 2 tablespoons sugar, the nutmeg, cinnamon, milk and egg until soft dough forms.

2 On surface sprinkled with additional Bisquick mix, roll dough into a ball; knead about 5 times. Press or roll dough to ½-inch thickness. Cut dough with doughnut cutter dipped in Bisquick mix. To make bow shapes, hold opposite sides of each ring of dough, then twist to make a figure 8. On ungreased cookie sheet, place bows and buttons (the dough from the center of each ring).

3 Bake 8 to 10 minutes or until light golden brown. Immediately dip each button and bow into melted butter, then into ½ cup sugar. Serve warm.

1 Button and Bow: Calories 250; Total Fat 10g (Saturated Fat 5g, Trans Fat 1.5g); Cholesterol 45mg; Sodium 420mg; Total Carbohydrate 36g (Dietary Fiber 0g); Protein 3g **Exchanges:** 1 Starch, 1½ Other Carbohydrate, 2 Fat **Carbohydrate Choices:** 2½

Strawberry–Cream Cheese Dough Knots

Prep Time: 20 Minutes • **Start to Finish:** 35 Minutes • Makes 8 knots

1 can (8 oz) refrigerated
crescent dinner rolls

¼ cup cream cheese spread

½ cup freeze-dried strawberry
slices

1 tablespoon butter, melted

½ cup powdered sugar

2 teaspoons hot water

Assorted colored sprinkles

1 Heat oven to 375°F. Unroll dough into 1 large rectangle. Firmly press perforations to seal. Shape into 12 x 8-inch rectangle. Cut crosswise into 8 strips (1½ x 8 inches each). Spread 1½ teaspoons cream cheese down center of each strip.

2 Top cream cheese with strawberry slices. (Break larger strawberry slices in half to fit on dough.) Fold dough over lengthwise to encase filling; press edge to seal in filling, forming each strip into long filled rope. Tie rope of dough into knot; place on large ungreased cookie sheet. Repeat with remaining 7 strips of dough. Brush knots with melted butter.

3 Bake 10 to 12 minutes or until golden brown. In small bowl, mix powdered sugar and hot water until smooth. Spread over each knot; top immediately with sprinkles. Serve warm.

1 Knot: Calories 210; Total Fat 10g (Saturated Fat 5g, Trans Fat 0g); Cholesterol 10mg; Sodium 260mg; Total Carbohydrate 27g (Dietary Fiber 1g); Protein 1g **Exchanges:** ½ Starch, 1½ Other Carbohydrate, 2 Fat **Carbohydrate Choices:** 2

Tip Freeze-drying strawberries is another method of dehydrating. Freeze-dried strawberries will be crispier and lighter because they contain less moisture than regular dried strawberries.

Churros

Prep Time: 35 Minutes • **Start to Finish:** 35 Minutes • Makes 30 churros

Vegetable oil for deep frying
4 tablespoons sugar
2 teaspoons ground cinnamon
3¼ cups Original Bisquick mix
1 cup hot water

1 In 3-quart saucepan, heat 2 to 3 inches oil to 375°F.

2 In small bowl, mix 3 tablespoons of the sugar and the cinnamon; set aside. In medium bowl, stir Bisquick mix, hot water and remaining 1 tablespoon sugar with spatula until dough forms.

3 Spoon dough into decorating bag fitted with ¼-inch star tip. Pipe 5-inch strips of dough into hot oil in batches. If necessary, cut dough with knife or scissors between each churro. Cook 2 to 3 minutes, turning frequently, until golden brown. Remove from oil with slotted spoon; drain on paper towels.

4 Immediately sprinkle generously with cinnamon-sugar mixture. Serve warm.

1 Churro: Calories 150; Total Fat 12g (Saturated Fat 2g, Trans Fat 0g); Cholesterol 0mg; Sodium 160mg; Total Carbohydrate 10g (Dietary Fiber 0g); Protein 1g **Exchanges:** ½ Starch, 2½ Fat **Carbohydrate Choices:** ½

Tip For a chocolate-covered delight, dip one end of each cooled churro into melted chocolate candy coating (almond bark), and place on waxed paper until set.

Lemon-Filled Doughnuts

Prep Time: 1 Hour 30 Minutes • **Start to Finish:** 4 Hours 25 Minutes • Makes 32 doughnuts

Doughnuts

1 cup warm milk (105°F to 115°F)

2 packages fast-acting dry yeast

4½ to 5 cups Gold Medal all-purpose flour

½ cup granulated sugar

1 teaspoon salt

3 eggs

⅓ cup butter, softened

Vegetable oil for deep frying

Filling

2 jars (10 oz each) lemon curd

Topping

1½ teaspoons powdered sugar

1 Pour warm milk into large bowl; stir in yeast until dissolved. Add 2 cups of the flour, the granulated sugar, salt, and eggs; mix with electric mixer on low speed 30 seconds, scraping bowl occasionally. Increase speed to medium; beat 2 minutes, scraping bowl occasionally. Add butter, 1 tablespoon at a time, mixing well after each addition. Stir in enough remaining flour, ½ cup at a time, to make dough easy to handle.

2 Place dough on lightly floured surface. Knead dough 2 minutes or until dough is smooth and springy. Grease large bowl with butter. Place dough in bowl, turning dough to grease all sides. Cover bowl with plastic wrap; let rise in warm place about 1 hour 45 minutes or until dough has doubled in size.

3 Sprinkle 2 cookie sheets with flour; set aside. Place dough on generously floured surface. Roll dough in flour to coat. With floured rolling pin, roll dough into 16 x 8-inch rectangle. Using sharp knife or pizza cutter, cut dough into 8 rows by 4 rows, forming 32 squares (doughnuts may be slightly uneven in shape, especially corners, since dough stretches when cut). On lightly floured surface, dust both sides of each doughnut with flour; place on cookie sheets about 2 inches apart. Loosely cover doughnuts with plastic wrap sprayed with cooking spray; let rise in warm place about 30 to 40 minutes or until slightly risen.

4 In 4-quart Dutch oven or heavy 3-quart saucepan, heat 2 inches oil to 325°F. Cover cooling rack with paper towels. Fry doughnuts in hot oil, 4 to 5 at a time, until golden brown on both sides, about 1 minute per side. Remove from oil with slotted spoon to cooling rack. Cool completely, about 30 minutes.

5 Place lemon curd in decorating bag fitted with writing tip (¼-inch opening). To fill each doughnut, while holding doughnut in hand, insert tip into side of doughnut. Slowly squeeze about 1 tablespoon lemon curd into center until you feel the doughnut plump up, moving tip from one side to the other to completely fill doughnut. Sprinkle with powdered sugar.

1 Doughnut: Calories 200; Total Fat 8g (Saturated Fat 2.5g, Trans Fat 0g); Cholesterol 40mg; Sodium 105mg; Total Carbohydrate 28g (Dietary Fiber 0g); Protein 3g **Exchanges:** 1 Starch, 1 Other Carbohydrate, 1½ Fat **Carbohydrate Choices:** 2

Tip You can make the dough the night before. Instead of letting it rise in a warm place for the first rise, place the covered bowl in the refrigerator up to 12 hours. Then continue as directed in recipe.

Beignets with Espresso Sugar

Prep Time: 50 Minutes · **Start to Finish:** 3 Hours 20 Minutes · Makes 30 beignets

Sugar Mixture

⅔ cup sugar

1 to 1¼ teaspoons espresso coffee powder

Beignets

2¾ cups Gold Medal all-purpose flour

¼ cup sugar

¼ teaspoon salt

1 package regular active or fast-acting dry yeast

¾ cup very warm milk (120°F to 130°F)

¼ cup butter or margarine, melted

1 teaspoon vanilla

2 eggs

Vegetable oil for deep frying

Glaze

⅓ cup dark, semisweet or milk chocolate chips

1 teaspoon vegetable oil

1 In small bowl, stir sugar mixture ingredients; set aside. Grease or spray large bowl with cooking spray; set aside.

2 Insert paddle attachment in electric stand mixer. In another large bowl, mix 2 cups of the flour, ¼ cup sugar, the salt and yeast. Add milk and butter. Beat on low speed 1 minute, scraping bowl and paddle frequently. Remove paddle attachment and insert dough hook. Add vanilla and eggs; beat until smooth. Beat on low speed 1 minute, scraping bowl and dough hook frequently. Stir in enough remaining flour to make dough easy to handle (dough will be slightly sticky).

3 Grease large bowl with shortening or cooking spray. Place dough in greased bowl, turning dough to grease all sides. Cover bowl with plastic wrap; let rise in warm place about 2 hours or until dough has doubled in size.

4 Sprinkle cookie sheet with flour; set aside. Place dough on generously floured surface. Roll dough in flour to coat. With floured rolling pin, roll dough to ½-inch thickness. Using 2-inch round cookie cutter, cut 30 rounds, gently pressing together and rerolling dough scraps as necessary. On lightly floured surface, sprinkle both sides of each round with flour; place on cookie sheet about 2 inches apart. Loosely cover beignets with plastic wrap sprayed with cooking spray; let rise in warm place 30 to 40 minutes or until slightly risen.

5 In 4-quart Dutch oven or 3-quart saucepan, heat 2 inches oil to 325°F. Cover cooling rack with paper towels. Fry beignets in hot oil, 4 to 5 at a time, until golden brown on both sides, about 1 minute per side. Remove from oil with slotted spoon to cooling rack. Immediately roll in sugar mixture.

6 Meanwhile, in small microwavable bowl, microwave chocolate chips on High 30 to 60 seconds, stirring once, until chips are softened and can be stirred smooth. Stir in 1 teaspoon oil until smooth. Spoon into small resealable food-storage plastic bag; seal bag. Cut off small corner of bag; squeeze bag to drizzle chocolate over each beignet.

1 Beignet: Calories 150; Total Fat 9g (Saturated Fat 2.5g, Trans Fat 0g); Cholesterol 15mg; Sodium 40mg; Total Carbohydrate 17g (Dietary Fiber 0g); Protein 2g **Exchanges:** 1 Starch, 1½ Fat **Carbohydrate Choices:** 1

Tip Frying only 4 to 5 beignets at a time helps to maintain the 325°F oil temperature. If you add more, the oil temperature drops too quickly and may result in under-cooked beignets.

Apple-Cinnamon Fritters

Prep Time: 25 Minutes • **Start to Finish:** 25 Minutes • Makes 22 fritters

Vegetable oil for deep frying

2 cups Original Bisquick mix

½ cup cold water

1 egg

¼ cup granulated sugar

1 teaspoon ground cinnamon

1 large unpeeled Granny Smith apple, chopped (about 1¾ cups)

¼ cup powdered sugar

1 In deep fryer or 4-quart heavy saucepan, heat 2 to 3 inches oil to 350°F.

2 In large bowl, stir Bisquick mix, water, egg, granulated sugar and cinnamon. Fold in apple. Carefully drop batter by tablespoonfuls into hot oil, a few at a time. Fry 2 to 3 minutes, turning occasionally, or until golden brown. Remove from oil with slotted spoon; drain on paper towels.

3 Sprinkle fritters with powdered sugar.

1 Fritter: Calories 70; Total Fat 1.5g (Saturated Fat 0g, Trans Fat 0g); Cholesterol 10mg; Sodium 135mg; Total Carbohydrate 12g (Dietary Fiber 0g); Protein 1g **Exchanges:** ½ Starch, ½ Other Carbohydrate **Carbohydrate Choices:** 1

Tip Use a melon baller or small ice cream scoop for measuring the batter and dropping into the oil.

Maple-Glazed Bacon Drop Doughnuts

Prep Time: 1 Hour 20 Minutes • **Start to Finish:** 1 Hour 20 Minutes • Makes 24 doughnut balls

Doughnuts

Vegetable oil for deep frying

1 egg

½ cup milk

2 tablespoons butter, melted

1½ cups all-purpose flour

¼ cup packed brown sugar

2 teaspoons baking powder

½ teaspoon salt

½ teaspoon ground cinnamon

6 slices maple-flavored bacon, crisply cooked, crumbled

Maple Glaze

3 cups powdered sugar

⅓ cup water

⅓ cup maple-flavored syrup

1 In 3-quart heavy saucepan or 4-quart Dutch oven, heat 2 inches oil to 350°F.

2 Meanwhile, in large bowl, beat egg, milk and butter with fork. Stir in flour, brown sugar, baking powder, salt, cinnamon and bacon.

3 Carefully drop dough by heaping tablespoonfuls, 6 at a time, into hot oil. Fry 30 seconds to 1 minute on each side, or until golden brown. Remove from oil with slotted spoon; drain on paper towels until cooled, about 20 minutes.

4 In medium bowl, mix powdered sugar and water until smooth; stir in maple-flavored syrup. Add additional water, 1 teaspoon at a time, until thick glaze consistency. Dip cooled doughnut balls into glaze; let excess drip off. (If glaze disappears while drying, glaze may be too thin. Try dipping balls again, or thicken up glaze by adding a small amount of powdered sugar.) Place glazed doughnut balls on cooling rack; let stand until glaze is set, about 10 minutes.

1 Doughnut Ball: Calories 180; Total Fat 7g (Saturated Fat 1.5g, Trans Fat 0g); Cholesterol 15mg; Sodium 150mg; Total Carbohydrate 27g (Dietary Fiber 0g); Protein 2g **Exchanges:** ½ Starch, 1½ Other Carbohydrate, 1½ Fat **Carbohydrate Choices:** 2

Tip Cook bacon quickly in the microwave. Place slices on microwavable plate lined with paper towels; cover with paper towel. Microwave on High 3 to 5 minutes or until crisp.

Aztec Chocolate Doughnuts

Prep Time: 1 Hour 10 Minutes • **Start to Finish:** 2 Hours 50 Minutes • Makes 16 doughnuts

Doughnuts

3 eggs

¾ cup granulated sugar

½ cup buttermilk

3 tablespoons butter, melted

1 teaspoon vanilla

¾ cup unsweetened baking cocoa

1¾ cups all-purpose flour

1½ teaspoons baking powder

¾ teaspoon ground cinnamon

½ teaspoon baking soda

½ teaspoon salt

Vegetable oil for deep frying

Chocolate Glaze

¼ cup butter

3 tablespoons milk

1 tablespoon light corn syrup

⅛ teaspoon ground cinnamon

¾ cup dark chocolate chips

1 to 1½ cups powdered sugar

1½ teaspoons vanilla

1 In medium bowl, beat eggs, granulated sugar, buttermilk, 3 tablespoons butter and 1 teaspoon vanilla with whisk until blended. Stir in cocoa. Stir in all remaining doughnut ingredients except oil just until moistened. Grease another medium bowl with shortening. Place dough in bowl, turning to grease all sides. Cover bowl with plastic wrap; refrigerate 1 hour.

2 Place dough on generously floured surface. Roll dough in flour to coat. With floured rolling pin, roll dough to ⅜-inch thickness. Cut dough with floured 3-inch cookie cutter.

3 Line 2 cookie sheets with cooking parchment paper. Place dough rounds on cookie sheets about 1 inch apart. Cut out centers using floured 1-inch cookie cutter. Reroll scraps to cut additional doughnuts. Cover cookie sheets loosely with towels; let stand at room temperature while heating oil.

4 In 4-quart Dutch oven or heavy 3-quart saucepan, heat 2 inches oil to 375°F. Place cooling rack on cookie sheet. Fry doughnuts in hot oil, 3 to 4 at a time, about 2 minutes, turning over every 30 seconds, until deep brown and puffed (do not undercook or centers will be raw). Remove from oil with slotted spoon to cooling rack. Cool doughnuts completely, about 20 minutes.

5 In 1½-quart microwavable bowl, microwave ¼ cup butter, milk, corn syrup and ⅛ teaspoon cinnamon on High 45 seconds or until mixture can be stirred smooth. Stir in chocolate chips. Microwave an additional 30 seconds; carefully stir until chocolate melts and mixture is smooth (stirring too quickly can cause air bubbles in glaze). Stir in 1 cup powdered sugar and the vanilla until smooth. Stir in additional powdered sugar, 1 tablespoon at a time, until consistency of thick syrup. Dip top of each doughnut into glaze; let excess drip off. Place doughnuts on cooling rack, allowing excess glaze to drip onto cookie sheet. Let stand until glaze is set, about 30 minutes.

1 Doughnut: Calories 290; Total Fat 14g (Saturated Fat 6g, Trans Fat 0g); Cholesterol 55mg; Sodium 220mg; Total Carbohydrate 36g (Dietary Fiber 2g); Protein 4g **Exchanges:** 1½ Starch, 1 Other Carbohydrate, 2½ Fat **Carbohydrate Choices:** 2½

Tip Try to maintain the temperature of the oil. Get oil back to 375°F before cooking each new batch of doughnuts. Turning the doughnuts frequently helps ensure that they cook thoroughly.

Cereal Crunch Doughnuts

Prep Time: 40 Minutes • **Start to Finish:** 40 Minutes • Makes 8 servings (1 doughnut and 1 hole each)

Use whatever cereal you like to top off these easy doughnuts!

1 In small bowl, stir chocolate glaze ingredients until smooth, adding enough milk for desired glaze consistency. Cover; set aside. In another small bowl, stir vanilla glaze ingredients until smooth, adding enough milk for desired glaze consistency. Cover; set aside.

2 In deep fryer or 4-quart heavy saucepan, heat 2 to 3 inches oil to 375°F.

3 Separate dough into 8 biscuits; cut hole in center of each. Fry biscuits and holes in hot oil 50 to 60 seconds on each side or until golden brown. Drain on paper towels.

4 Dip top of each doughnut and hole into desired glaze. Top with cereal. Serve warm.

1 Serving: Calories 350; Total Fat 18g (Saturated Fat 4g, Trans Fat 3.5g); Cholesterol 0mg; Sodium 620mg; Total Carbohydrate 44g (Dietary Fiber 0g); Protein 3g **Exchanges:** 1 Starch, 2 Other Carbohydrate, 3½ Fat **Carbohydrate Choices:** 3

Tip Don't be afraid to deep-fry—it's easy! Just be sure to maintain the correct oil temperature so that the outside gets crisp and golden brown and the inside stays tender. One of the secrets of success is to fry the doughnuts in batches to keep from overcrowding the pan and causing a drop in the oil temperature.

Chocolate Glaze
½ cup powdered sugar

1 tablespoon unsweetened baking cocoa

1 tablespoon butter, melted

3 to 4 teaspoons milk

Vanilla Glaze
½ cup powdered sugar

2 to 3 teaspoons milk

Donuts
Vegetable oil for deep frying

1 can (16.3 oz) refrigerated large buttermilk or original biscuits

Topping
1 cup Trix®, Reese's® Puffs® or Cocoa Puffs® cereal

Metric Conversion Guide

Volume

U.S. Units	Canadian Metric	Australian Metric
¼ teaspoon	1 mL	1 ml
½ teaspoon	2 mL	2 ml
1 teaspoon	5 mL	5 ml
1 tablespoon	15 mL	20 ml
¼ cup	50 mL	60 ml
⅓ cup	75 mL	80 ml
½ cup	125 mL	125 ml
⅔ cup	150 mL	170 ml
¾ cup	175 mL	190 ml
1 cup	250 mL	250 ml
1 quart	1 liter	1 liter
1½ quarts	1.5 liters	1.5 liters
2 quarts	2 liters	2 liters
2½ quarts	2.5 liters	2.5 liters
3 quarts	3 liters	3 liters
4 quarts	4 liters	4 liters

Weight

U.S. Units	Canadian Metric	Australian Metric
1 ounce	30 grams	30 grams
2 ounces	55 grams	60 grams
3 ounces	85 grams	90 grams
4 ounces (¼ pound)	115 grams	125 grams
8 ounces (½ pound)	225 grams	225 grams
16 ounces (1 pound)	455 grams	500 grams
1 pound	455 grams	0.5 kilogram

Note: The recipes in this cookbook have not been developed or tested using metric measures. When converting recipes to metric, some variations in quality may be noted.

Measurements

Inches	Centimeters
1	2.5
2	5.0
3	7.5
4	10.0
5	12.5
6	15.0
7	17.5
8	20.5
9	23.0
10	25.5
11	28.0
12	30.5
13	33.0

Temperatures

Fahrenheit	Celsius
32°	0°
212°	100°
250°	120°
275°	140°
300°	150°
325°	160°
350°	180°
375°	190°
400°	200°
425°	220°
450°	230°
475°	240°
500°	260°

Recipe Testing and Calculating Nutrition Information

Recipe Testing:

- Large eggs and 2% milk were used unless otherwise indicated.
- Fat-free, low-fat, low-sodium or lite products were not used unless indicated.
- No nonstick cookware and bakeware were used unless otherwise indicated. No dark-colored, black or insulated bakeware was used.
- When a pan is specified, a metal pan was used; a baking dish or pie plate means ovenproof glass was used.
- An electric hand mixer was used for mixing only when mixer speeds are specified.

Calculating Nutrition:

- The first ingredient was used wherever a choice is given, such as ⅓ cup sour cream or plain yogurt.
- The first amount was used wherever a range is given, such as 3- to 3½-pound whole chicken.
- The first serving number was used wherever a range is given, such as 4 to 6 servings.
- "If desired" ingredients were not included.
- Only the amount of a marinade or frying oil that is absorbed was included.